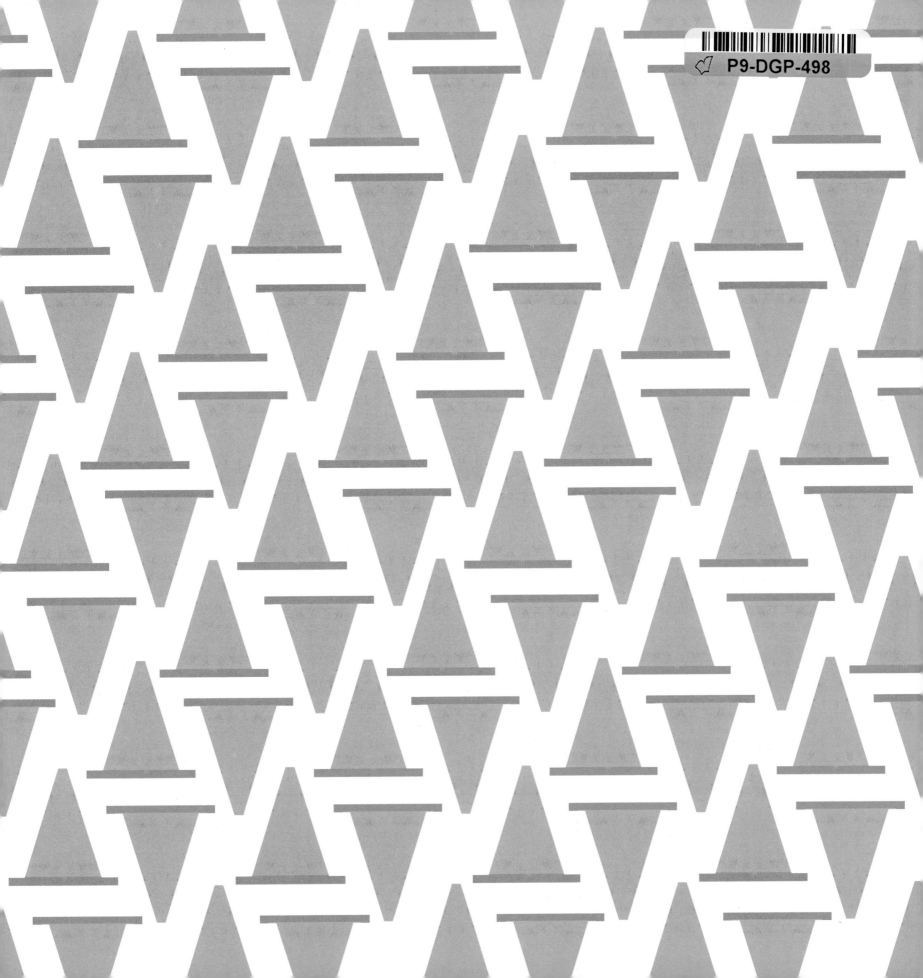

on the
construction
site

Carron Brown

Illustrated by Bee Johnson

Kane Miller
A DIVISION OF EDC PUBLISHING

A tall skyscraper is being built.

If you look closely around the construction site, through the steel beams and the concrete, you will find machines and people hard at work.

Shine a flashlight behind the page, or hold it up to a light to reveal what is hidden in and around the construction site. Discover a world of great surprises.

People will live in this skyscraper
when it's finished. Can you see the plans?

Architects and engineers work together to design the building. The plans show what it will look like.

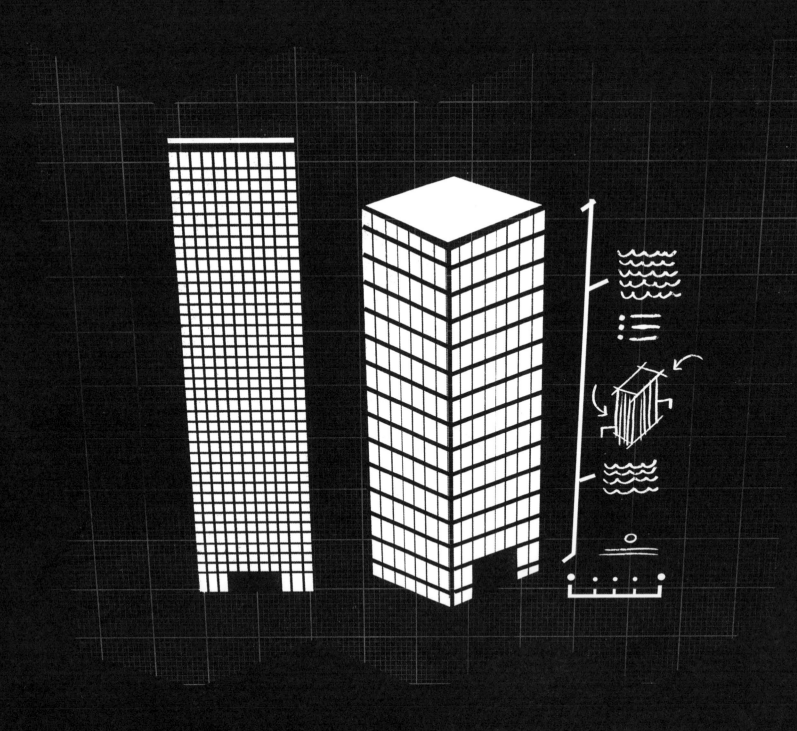

People watch as the area is cleared.

What is this truck taking away?

Rumble!

This dump truck is full of rocks and rubble.
The back lifts up and tips to dump the load.

Tall buildings need to stand on strong, solid ground. This means builders have to dig down to make the foundations. How many diggers can you see?

There is a digger in the pit
as well as on the surface.
Their claws scoop out earth
to make a huge hole.

Scrape!

The skyscraper's foundations
are very, very deep.

What is this
machine doing?

A pile driver is
hammering steel
poles into the bedrock.

Steel is a strong metal.

Bang!

Bang!

This cement mixer is making concrete for the foundations. What's going on inside it?

Whoosh!
Swoosh!

Water and cement whirl around and around in the drum.
They mix together to make concrete.

The foundations are leveled, ready for the concrete that forms the basement floor.

Can you see which machines smooth out the ground?

Bulldozers push earth aside to finish the foundations.
They have flat tracks instead of wheels.

Sweep!

Sweep!

The frame of the skyscraper is built next. Workers on the ground guide crane operators who place the steel beams.

Can you see how they talk to each other?

The crane operator
follows hand signals.

Each signal means
something different.

Down!

Down!

An ironworker is fixing the beam in place.

Can you see how?

Sizzle!

Crackle!

Metal melts at
high temperatures.
The ironworker welds,
or joins, the beams by
melting them together
with a welding torch.

Floors are added to the metal frame.

A layer of thin steel sheeting is
laid onto the beams.

What is added next?

Concrete is poured onto the floor.
It will dry hard and flat.

Carpets will be added after
the walls have been painted.

Skoosh!

Materials are needed at the top of the building.

How do they get there?

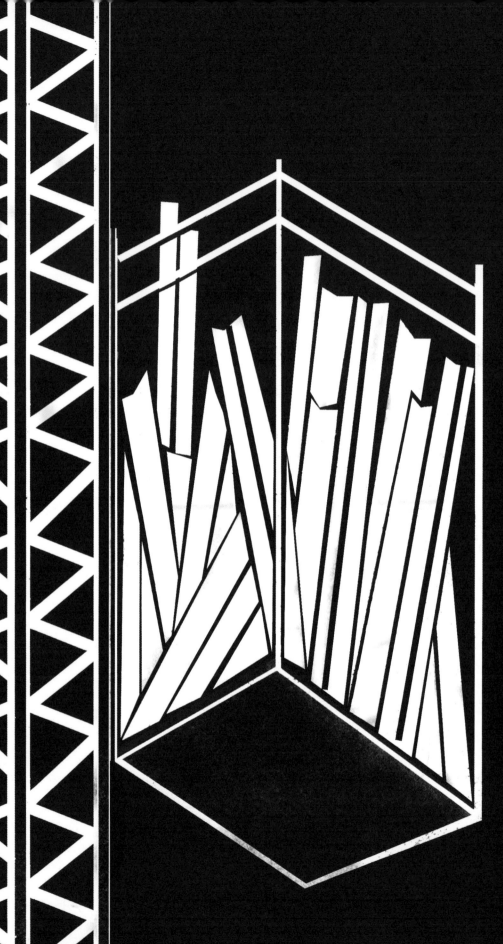

Up!
Up!
Up!

A hoist full
of steel beams
goes up the
tall tower like
an elevator.

The tower is
joined to the
building to
keep it safe
and steady.

Glass is placed on the outside
of the building.

Can you see who's inside?

Busy,
busy, busy. . .

There are a lot of
builders at work.

The glass is tinted to
shelter the people inside

Plumbers and electricians are adding water and electrical systems to the finished floors.

Where are the pipes and wires?

The pipes and wires are
hidden behind the walls
and under the floor.

Buzzz!

A heavy steamroller drives over fresh asphalt to make a flat road.

What is under the asphalt?

Crunch!

The road is made of
many layers.

There is earth, sand, and
gravel under the asphalt.

The road is soon being
used by lots of people.

What is inside
the trucks?

One truck has a ladder, paint, and brushes to decorate the apartments.

The other trucks have lots of boxes and furniture. Can you guess why?

On the top floor, a family moves
into their new home.

132

What will
the view be
like?

Wow!

The skyscraper is complete, and now people live here.

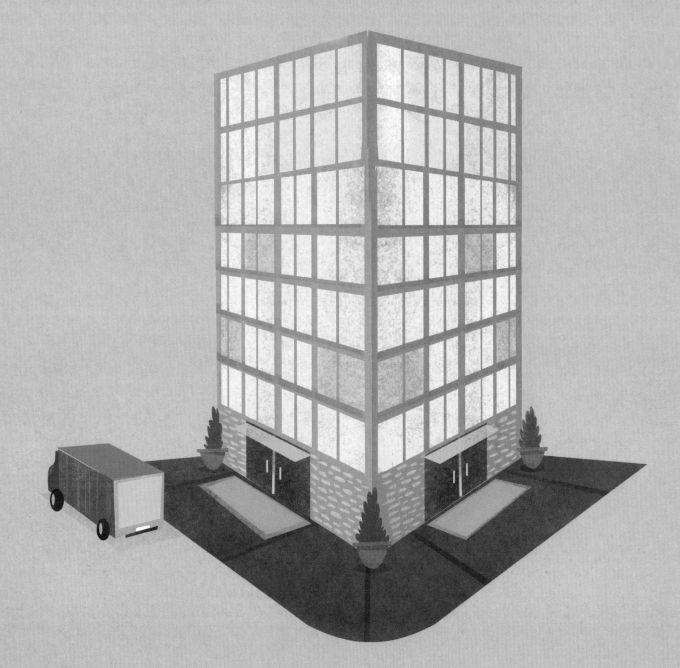

The workers and machines have moved to
another site, ready to build again.

There's more...

The next time you see a construction site, find the different machines and the job each one is doing.

Digger Some diggers have a long arm, called a boom, with a bucket at the end. The arm lowers the bucket so it can scoop up the soil. The boom lifts the bucket and empties the soil into a dump truck.

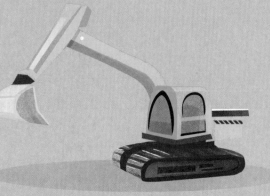

Dump truck The big container can be filled with soil and rubble. Pumps called pistons lift it up near the front and tilt it backward. The back flap, called a tailgate, opens and the container empties.

Pile driver This machine works like a giant hammer. A heavy weight at the end of its arm lifts and drops to push a steel or concrete pole (called a pile) into the ground.

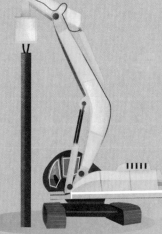

Cement mixer The big drum is turned by a motor to mix the water, cement, and stones inside it. The drum keeps turning to stop the concrete mix from setting.

Bulldozer The large metal blade on the front can be moved up and down by a lever in the cab. It makes the ground level by pushing the soil in front of it.

Crane This machine lifts loads up, down, and from side to side. A long, straight arm called a beam turns on one spot. A long cable hangs from the beam. It winds around a wheel called a pulley to lift objects at the end of the cable.

Hoist A hoist is a cage that carries materials up and down the outside of a building, like an elevator. The cage travels along a straight metal pole and is powered by a motor.

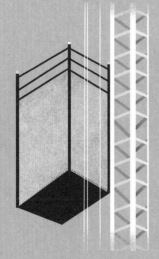

Steamroller A steamroller uses one or more heavy metal wheels called rollers to flatten a road surface. The largest rollers can weigh as much as a small jet plane!

First American Edition 2015
Kane Miller, A Division of EDC Publishing

Copyright © 2015 by The Ivy Press Limited

Published by arrangement with Ivy Press Limited, United Kingdom.

For information, contact:
Kane Miller, A Division of EDC Publishing
PO Box 470663
Tulsa, OK 74147-0663
www.kanemiller.com
www.edcpub.com
www.usbornebooksandmore.com

Library of Congress Control Number: 2014950265

Printed in China

2 3 4 5 6 7 8 9 10

ISBN: 978-1-61067-370-9